DVD
VIDEO
INCLUDED

ACOUSTIC
GUITAR CHORDS

BY CHAD JOHNSON

T0071701

ISBN 978-1-4584-0029-1

HAL•LEONARD®
CORPORATION

7777 W. BLUEMOUND RD. P.O. BOX 13819 MILWAUKEE, WI 53213

In Australia Contact:
Hal Leonard Australia Pty. Ltd.
4 Lentara Court
Cheltenham, Victoria, 3192 Australia
Email: ausadmin@halleonard.com.au

Visit Hal Leonard Online at
www.halleonard.com

Introduction

Welcome to *Acoustic Guitar Chords*. This book will teach you the chords you need to be a well-rounded acoustic guitar player. The aim is to get you jamming quickly, so we won't get bogged down in too many details. This is not a comprehensive method. Rather, it concentrates on the chord shapes that have stood the test of time and appear in countless songs.

You'll find that some of these chords will sound best strummed, whereas others may lend themselves to a more fingerstyle approach. However, feel free to experiment in this regard. Many a player's style has been crafted by approaching the same material in a fresh, new way. So grab your guitar and let's get to it.

About the DVD

The DVD that accompanies this book is a powerful teaching tool. It contains audio/visual examples of every chord covered. The chords are first strummed and then plucked string-by-string, so you can hear each individual note and make sure you've got it right. Also, each chord progression is demonstrated with a full band accompaniment so you can hear these chords in the proper context. Tuning notes are also included on the DVD.

Chord grids are provided for many of the examples in the book—especially after a chord type is first introduced—but eventually you'll figure out where they are on your own. The neck diagram in the Appendix will be your guide here, but also remember that you can see every chord form used in each example on the DVD as well.

Table of Contents

How to Read Chord Diagrams

The chords in this book are presented in chord diagram (or chord grid) fashion. The six vertical lines represent the strings; the lowest pitched (thickest) string is on the left, and the highest pitched (thinnest) is on the right.

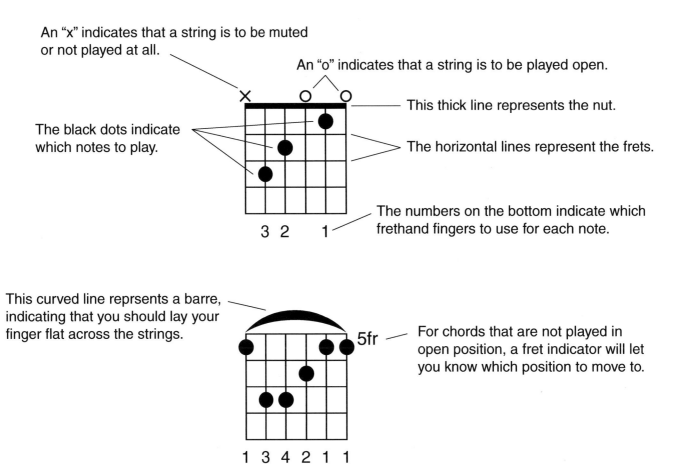

An "x" indicates that a string is to be muted or not played at all.

An "o" indicates that a string is to be played open.

This thick line represents the nut.

The black dots indicate which notes to play.

The horizontal lines represent the frets.

The numbers on the bottom indicate which frethand fingers to use for each note.

This curved line reprsents a barre, indicating that you should lay your finger flat across the strings.

For chords that are not played in open position, a fret indicator will let you know which position to move to.

A Brief Chord Theory Primer

Chords are built from intervals, or degrees, of notes from a major (or minor) scale. A major scale contains seven notes, and those notes are numbered 1 through 7. (The 1 is also commonly referred to as the "root" or "tonic.") So if a chord contains the root, 3rd, and 5th, then it contains the 1st, 3rd, and 5th notes of the root's major scale. If it contains a root, ♭3rd, and 5th, then the 3rd is lowered by a half step. This is referred to as a chord's *formula*. The formula for each type of chord in this book is given.

In order to understand how the chords in this book are built, you simply need to know all twelve major scales, which are found in the Appendix, and apply the formula to a particular root note.

For example, the formula for a major chord is root, 3rd, 5th (or 1–3–5). If you want to understand how a C major chord is built, you would look in the Appendix to find the C major scale. Its notes are C–D–E–F–G–A–B (no sharps or flats). Take the 1st (C), 3rd (E), and 5th (G) notes, and you have the chord. A C major chord is spelled C–E–G.

The formula for a minor chord is 1–♭3–5. So, to build a Cm chord, you would only have to lower the 3rd note (E) down a half step to E♭. So a Cm chord is spelled C–E♭–G. You can use this method to determine the spelling of any chord presented in this book.

OPEN CHORDS

Let's start with open major and minor chords, or *triads*. Triads are made up of three notes: a root, a 3rd, and 5th. The formula for a major chord is 1–3–5; a minor chord's formula is 1–♭3–5. These are *open* chords because they contain one or more open strings.

Major Chords

Here's our first major chord: E major.

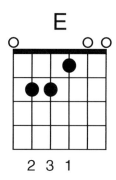

Here's A major.

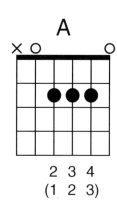

And here's a D major chord.

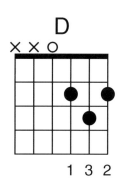

Note that when a chord name consists of only a capital letter (such as E or A), it's implied that it's a major chord.

Now let's hear what these chords sound like in action. When we play a series of chords, as in a song, we're playing a *chord progression*.

Example 1

In this next example, we're switching chords every two beats. This means you'll really need to have those chord shapes down cold.

Example 2

You'll hear *syncopation* in the strum pattern of this next example. This is just a fancy word for accenting the weak beat, or upbeat. You create this accent by varying the force with which you strum. The accented strums will be the loudest, some will be moderate in volume, and still others in between may be very quiet.

Example 3

Let's learn a few more open major chords.

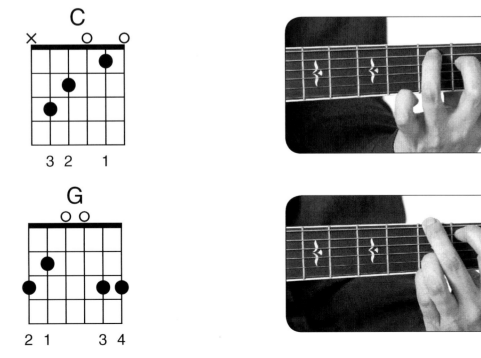

A popular variation on the G chord leaves the B string open and uses the a 3–2–4 fingering, low to high. This version is often paired with a C chord because they share a similar fingering.

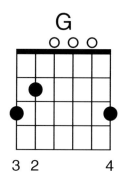

Feel free to experiment with both G chord voicings throughout your studies. You might find, for example, that the first version transitions easily to a D chord, because the third finger remains in place for both chords.

And now let's hear how these new chords sound.

Example 4

You don't always have to strum these chords either. You can also pluck through the notes individually, which is called an *arpeggio*. Here's what the same chord progression sounds like when we arpeggiate the chords.

Example 5

You can create a nice texture by leaving lots of space too, as in this next example.

Example 6

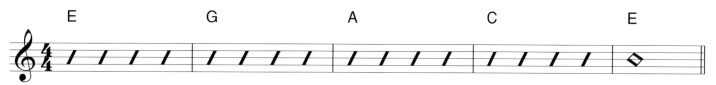

Minor Chords

Now let's look at some minor chords. These have a dark, sad quality compared to a major chord's bright, happy sound.

Em

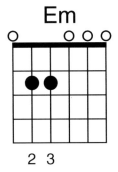

2 3

Am

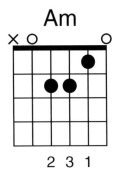

2 3 1

Dm

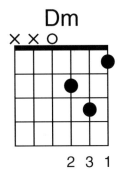

2 3 1

A chord symbol for a minor chord contains the suffix "m" after the capital letter.

Notice that each one of these chords differs from the same major chord by only one note. That note is the chord's 3rd. Remember: minor chords are the same as major, except the 3rd is flatted (lowered by a half step).

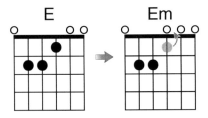

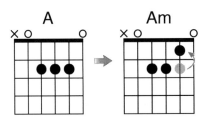

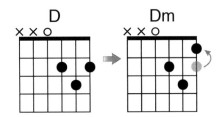

Here's a chord progression that uses some minor chords.

Example 7

This next example is in 12/8, which means four "beats" counted in groups of three, like this:

1 2 3, **4** 5 6, **7** 8 9, **10** 11 12.

Example 8

Most songs are made up of combinations of major and minor chords. Notice in this example how the G and C chords are embellished with quick hammer-ons with the first and second finger, respectively. In the case of the G chord, you strum through the chord with the fifth string open and then quickly hammer down onto the second fret with your first finger. The C chord uses the same concept, but your second finger hammers onto the second fret of the fourth string.

Example 9

In this next example, try using the *palm mute* technique. As you pick, lay your palm on the strings where they meet the bridge. You'll get a choked, muffled sound. You can apply and release the technique to get a dynamic sound.

Example 10

BARRE CHORDS

Barre chords are usually the most difficult to master, because they require the most hand strength. There are two main barre chord forms commonly used: the 6th-string form and the 5th-string form.

Major Barre Chords

6th-String Form

Here, you'll be barring across all six strings with your first finger. This is sometimes called an "E-form" because it resembles an open E chord.

5th-String Form

In this form, you're barring across three strings with your third finger. This is sometimes called an "A-form" because it resembles an open A chord.

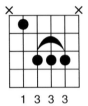

If you play the 6th-string form with your first finger on the third fret, you have a G chord.

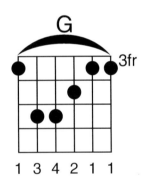

If you play the 5th-string form with your first finger on the third fret, you have a C chord.

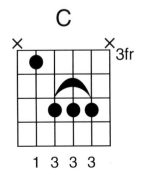

You can move these forms anywhere along either one of these strings to play different chords. (Refer to the neck diagram in the Appendix for the names of all the notes on the fretboard.)

This example uses all 6th-string forms. Notice how we're deliberately sliding from chord to chord to create a lazy effect.

Example 11

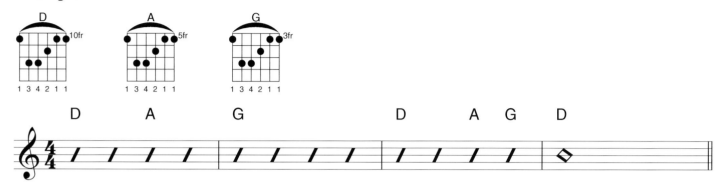

And here we're moving only the 5th-string form around.

Example 12

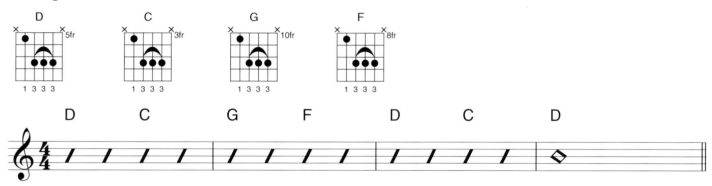

Now let's combine the forms. In this example, listen for the *scratch rhythm technique*. It's accomplished by laying your frethand fingers lightly on the strings to mute them (but not pushing down) and strumming to create a percussive effect.

Example 13

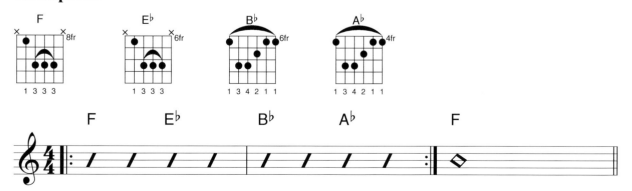

Minor Barre Chords

As with the open chords, the minor barre chords differ only from the major ones by one note.

6th-String Form

1 3 4 1 1 1

5th-String Form

This is slightly different than its major counterpart; here, you're barring five strings with your first finger.

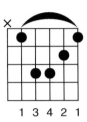

1 3 4 2 1

Again, you'll see these referred to as E-forms and A-forms, respectively. If you play the 6th-string form with your first finger on the third fret, you have a Gm chord.

Gm

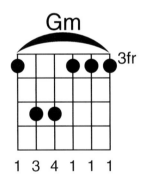

3fr

1 3 4 1 1 1

If you play the 5th-string form with your first finger on the third fret, you have a Cm chord.

Cm

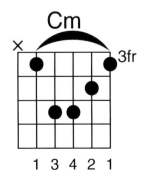

3fr

1 3 4 2 1

Let's move around the 6th-string form for this example. We're using a shuffle feel here. This gives the notes a lopsided feel. Think of a blues song like "Pride and Joy" or "Tore Down," and you're hearing a shuffle feel.

Example 14

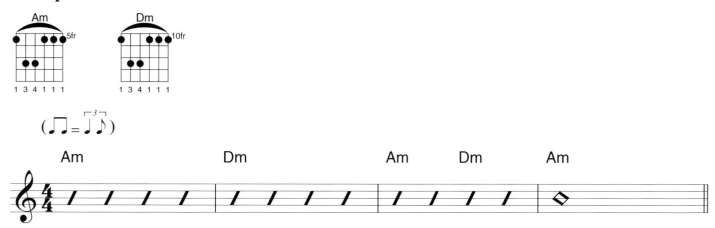

This one uses the 5th-string form, arpeggiating through the chords with a shuffle feel. Notice the alternate fingering for the open Am chord. This is done so that you don't have to change fingerings from the Am back to the Dm. It also helps to illustrate how these barre forms are truly derived from the open chords. In the case of this Am, you can think of the nut as the barre.

Example 15

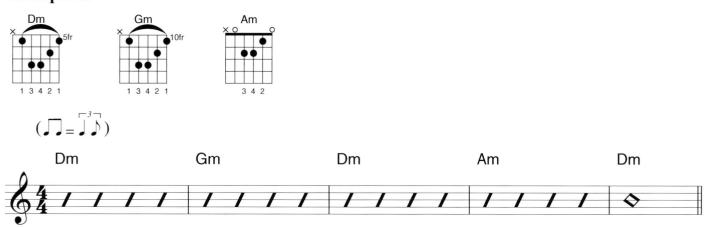

And now we'll combine both forms.

Example 16

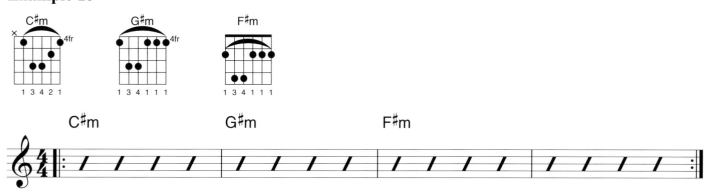

Now let's combine our major and minor barre chord shapes in both forms.

Example 17

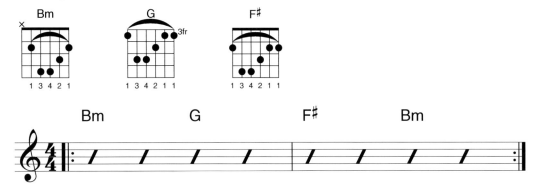

This example is played fingerstyle, with the thumb plucking strings 5 or 6 and the index, middle, and ring fingers plucking strings 4, 3, and 2.

Example 18

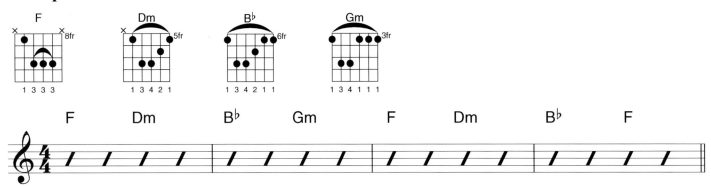

Example 19

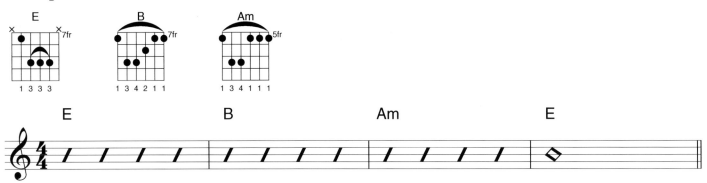

We use fingerstyle in this example as well. For the final Cm chord, strum through the strings with your thumb.

Example 20

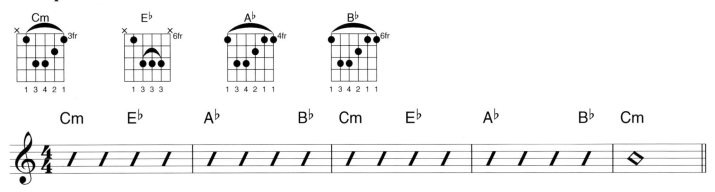

SEVENTH CHORDS

A *seventh chord* has four different notes: a root, 3rd, 5th, and 7th. There are many different types, but we'll look at the two most commonly found in rock: the dominant 7th (1–3–5–♭7) and the minor 7th (1–♭3–5–♭7).

Dominant Seventh Chords

Dominant seventh chords sound bluesy and funky. They contain a major 3rd like a major chord, but the ♭7th makes them sound less stable and a bit tougher.

Open Forms

E7

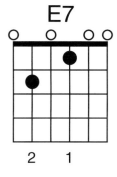

A7

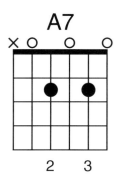

D7

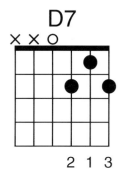

G7

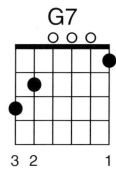

C7

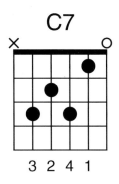

×   O

3 2 4 1

B7

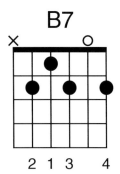

×   O

2 1 3 4

6th-String Barre Form

1 3 1 2 1 1

5th-String Barre Form

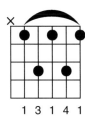

×

1 3 1 4 1

If you play the 6th-string form with your first finger on the third fret, you have a G7 chord.

G7

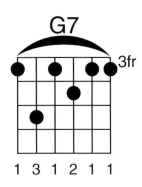

3fr

1 3 1 2 1 1

If you play the 5th-string form with your first finger on the third fret, you have a C7 chord.

C7

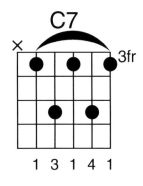

×   3fr

1 3 1 4 1

Now let's incorporate dominant seventh chords into some chord progressions. For this first example, use all barre chords. (Again, refer to the Appendix if you can't remember the notes on the 6th and 5th strings.)

Example 21

This example is played with all open forms.

Example 22

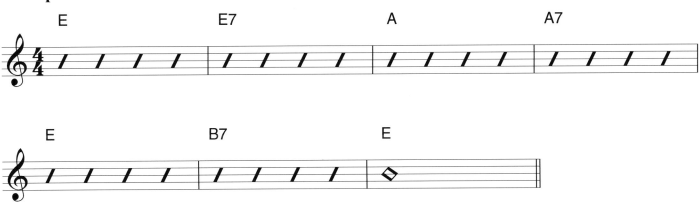

And here's a 12-bar blues in the key of A. In the blues, it's common to use all dominant seventh chords. Use barre forms for the A7 and D7 and an open E7 chord.

Example 23

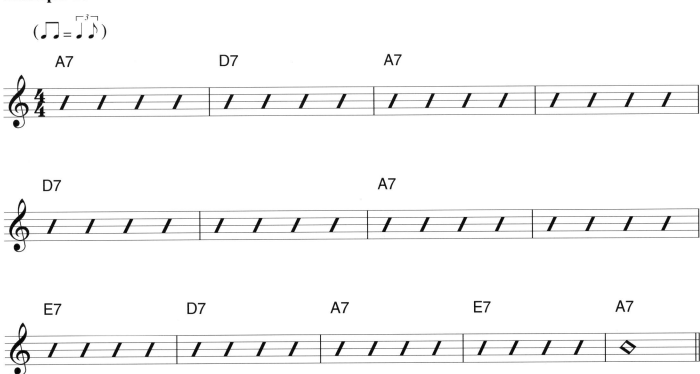

Minor Seventh Chords

Minor seventh chords sound a little more sophisticated or jazzy than minor chords. They're usually interchangeable with minor chords (triads), so experiment with them to hear the different effect they create.

Open Forms

Em7

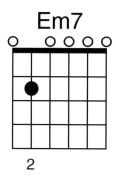

Am7

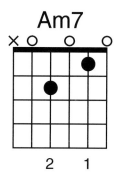

Dm7

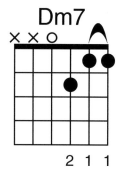

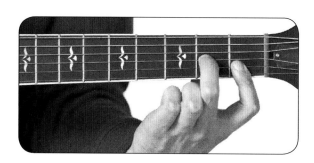

Bm7*

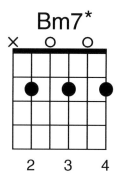

*This open Bm7 form is used much less frequently than the open B7 form.

Notice that these forms differ from the dominant forms by one note only. The 3rd of each dominant chord is lowered to create a minor seventh chord. (Cm7 doesn't appear as an open form because the 3rd of C7, E, is lowered to $E\flat$, which is not an open string.)

6th-String Barre Form

1 3 1 1 1 1

5th-String Barre Form

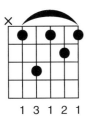

1 3 1 2 1

If you play the 6th-string form with your first finger on the third fret, you have a Gm7 chord.

Gm7

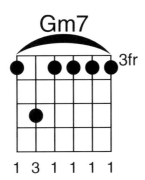

3fr

1 3 1 1 1 1

If you play the 5th-string form with your first finger on the third fret, you have a Cm7 chord.

Cm7

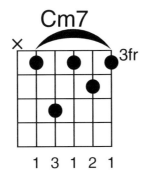

3fr

1 3 1 2 1

Let's incorporate minor seventh chords into some progressions. This first one uses all open forms.

Example 24

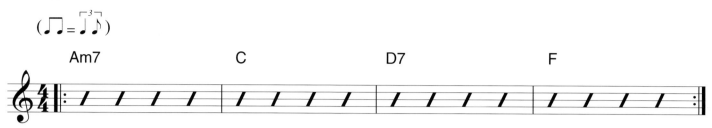

For this example, use barre chords throughout, referencing the neck diagram in the Appendix if necessary.

Example 25

This next example is a 12-bar minor blues in the key of A. In a minor blues, it's common to use all minor seventh and dominant seventh chords. We'll use all barre forms in this one.

Example 26

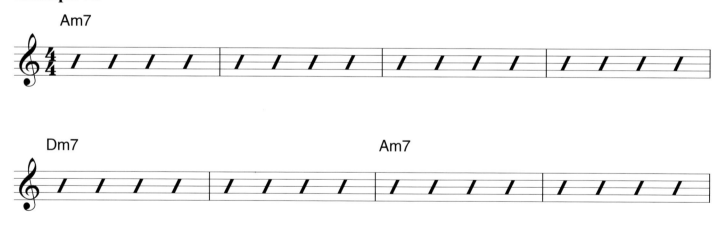

OTHER CHORD TYPES

Besides triads and seventh chords, there are others that occur often as well. Let's learn a few of these.

Suspended Chords

Suspended chords are somewhat ambiguous and open sounding because they don't have a 3rd. However, they are still three-note chords; the 3rd is simply replaced by either a 2nd or a 4th. The former results in a sus2 chord (1–2–5), and the latter results in a sus4 chord (1–4–5).

Open Forms

Esus4

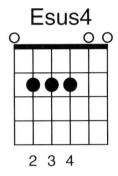

2 3 4

Asus2

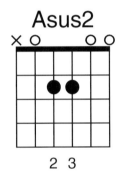

2 3

Asus4

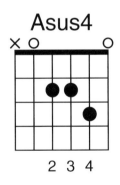

2 3 4

Dsus2

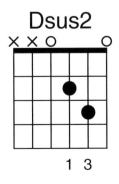

1 3

Dsus4

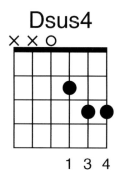

X X O

1 3 4

6th-String Barre Form

suspended 4th

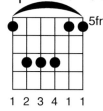

5fr

1 2 3 4 1 1

If you play the 6th-string form with your first finger on the third fret, you have a Gsus4 chord.

Gsus4

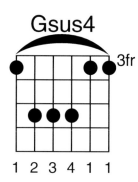

3fr

1 2 3 4 1 1

Suspended 2nd barre chords based off a 6th-string root aren't typically used.

5th-String Barre Forms

suspended 4th

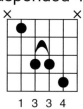

X   X

1 3 3 4

suspended 2nd

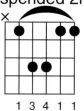

X

1 3 4 1 1

If you play the 5th-string forms with your first finger on the third fret, you have a Csus4 chord and a Csus2 chord.

Csus4

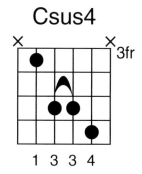

X   X 3fr

1 3 3 4

Csus2

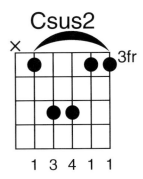

×   3fr

1 3 4 1 1

Suspended chords are often (though not always) interchangeable with their major and minor counterparts. They also often resolve to (are followed by) their major or minor counterparts. For example, Dsus2 or Dsus4 will often be followed by D (or Dm).

Add Nine Chords

Add nine chords (add9) have a lush quality that can be just what's needed to give an extra lift to a chord progression. They can either be major (1–3–5–9) or minor (1–♭3–5–9). (The 9th interval is the same as the 2nd, only an octave higher.) Add nine chords are generally interchangeable with major or minor chords.

Open Forms

Eadd9

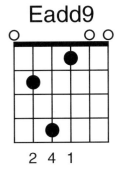

2 4 1

Em(add9)

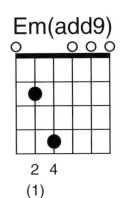

2 4

(1)

Aadd9

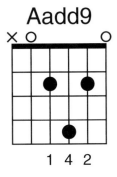

1 4 2

Am(add9)

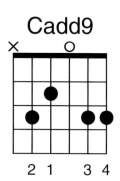

2 4 1

Cadd9

2 1   3 4

Cadd9 (alternate)

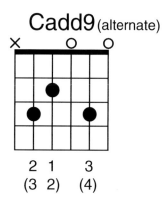

2 1   3
(3 2) (4)

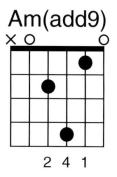

Notice that there are two commonly used versions of Cadd9. The first one is very often alternated with a G chord (the four-finger version).

Barre Forms

6th-String Forms

major add9

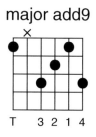

T   3 2 1 4

minor add9

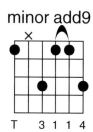

T   3 1 1 4

The thumb (indicated by "T") is optional in these forms. You can also just play the top four strings.

If you play the 6th-string forms with your thumb on the third fret, you have Gadd9 and Gm(add9) chords.

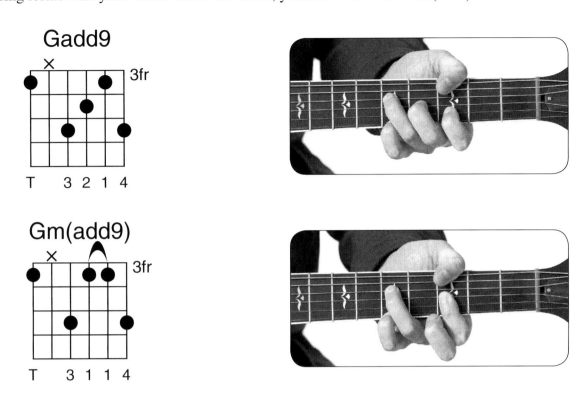

Gadd9

Gm(add9)

Barre forms of add9 chords based off a 5th-string root aren't typically used.

Let's hear how some of these chord forms can dress up a standard progression. Try to let the arpeggios ring out as much as possible in this example.

Example 27

Eadd9   Asus2   C♯sus2   F♯add9   E

Example 28

Dsus4   D   Asus4   A   Cadd9   Gadd9 Gm(add9)   D

Sus2 chords are sometimes moved around and used for every chord in a progression, as is the case with this fingerstyle example.

Example 29

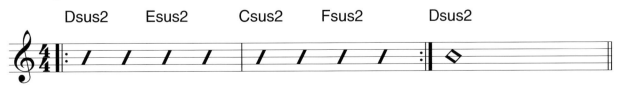

Dsus2   Esus2   Csus2   Fsus2   Dsus2

Another common device, especially with acoustic guitar, is the use of open strings with chords that aren't played in open position. It's very common, for instance, to move the fretted notes of open chords, such as E, C, D, etc., up the neck while still allowing the open strings to ring out—acting as drones in a sense. You can get some very colorful sounds this way.

There really is no rule with this concept; it's open to experimentation. However, here are some of the more common concoctions.

Based Off Open E Chord

G6/E

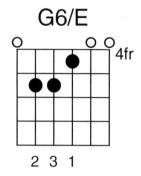

4fr

2 3 1

Aadd9/E

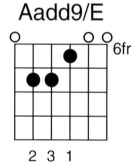

6fr

2 3 1

Badd4/E

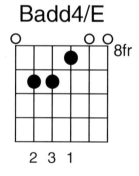

8fr

2 3 1

Based Off Open A Chord

Badd4/A

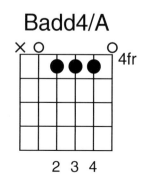

4fr

2 3 4

Am7

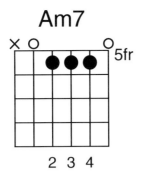

× O ○ 5fr

2 3 4

Dadd9/A

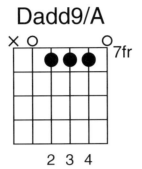

× O ○ 7fr

2 3 4

Based Off Open C Chord

Dadd$_9^4$

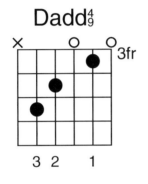

× O O 3fr

3 2 1

Fmaj9

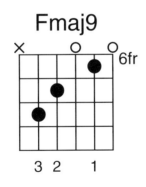

× O O 6fr

3 2 1

G6

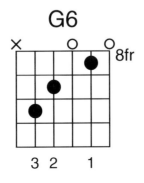

× O O 8fr

3 2 1

Based Off Open D Chord

E/D

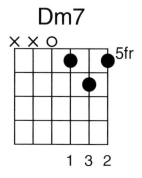

× × O   4fr

1 3 2

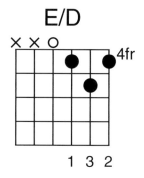

Dm7

× × O   5fr

1 3 2

A/D

× × O   9fr

1 3 2

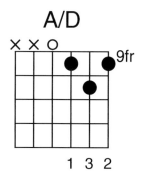

SONG EXAMPLES

Now let's play a few full songs that make use of everything we've covered. The DVD will show you which chord forms are used, but feel free to experiment with your own choices for a different sound.

This is a pop rock tune in G that uses mostly strumming, but listen for a few arpeggios here and there.

Example 30

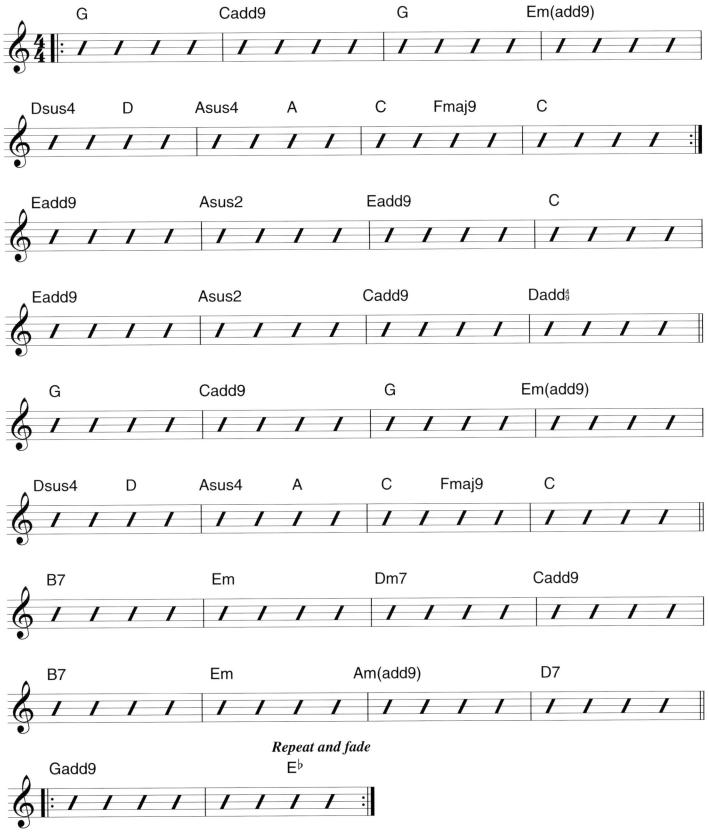

Here's a shuffle tune in D that makes use of lots of sevenths and barre chords.

Example 31

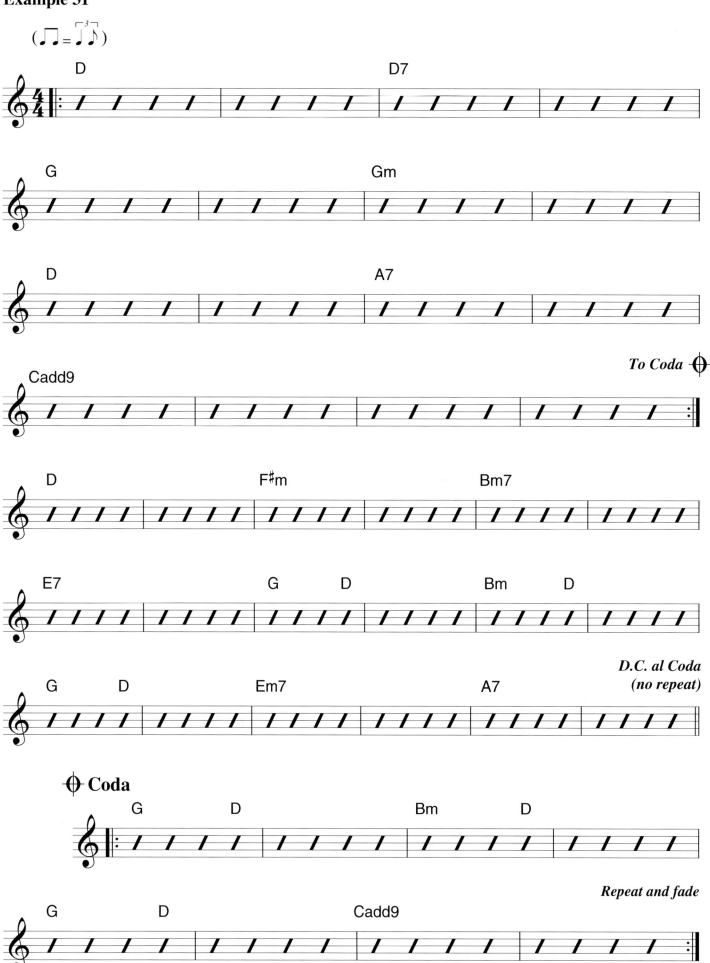

This final example is a fingerstyle ballad in the key of E. This uses the "backbeat" technique to enhance the groove. On beats 2 and 4, plant your right hand forcefully down on the strings in preparation for the next chord. The effect is that of a snare drum and is especially effective when playing in a solo setting or small ensemble.

Example 32

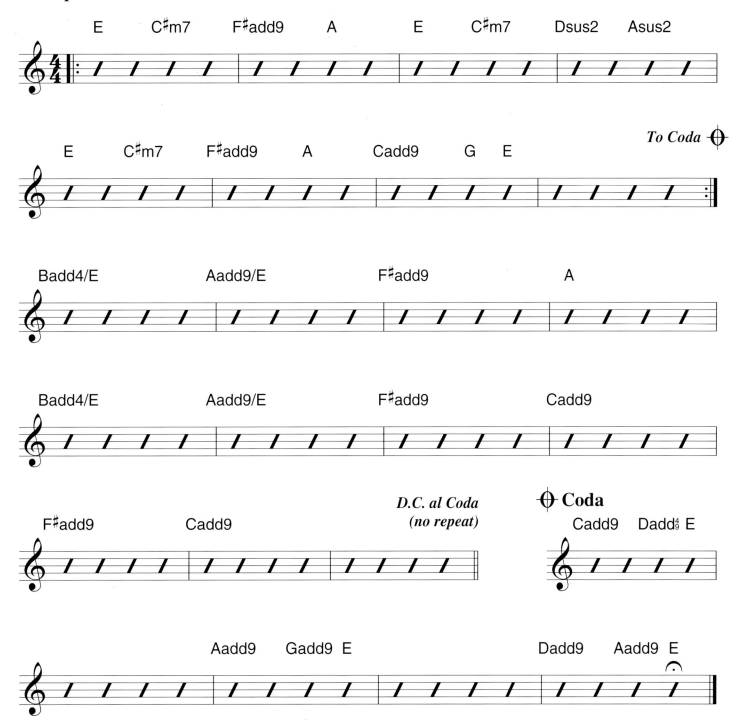

Appendix

Neck Diagram

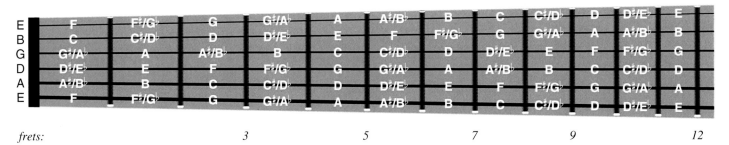

frets: *3*   *5*   *7*   *9*   *12*

Twelve Major Scales

C Major: C–D–E–F–G–A–B

G Major: G–A–B–C–D–E–F$\sharp$

D Major: D–E–F$\sharp$–G–A–B–C$\sharp$

A Major: A–B–C$\sharp$–D–E–F$\sharp$–G$\sharp$

E Major: E–F$\sharp$–G$\sharp$–A–B–C$\sharp$–D$\sharp$

B Major: B–C$\sharp$–D$\sharp$–E–F$\sharp$–G$\sharp$–A$\sharp$

F Major: F–G–A–B$\flat$–C–D–E

B$\flat$ Major: B$\flat$–C–D–E$\flat$–F–G–A

E$\flat$ Major: E$\flat$–F–G–A$\flat$–B$\flat$–C–D

A$\flat$ Major: A$\flat$–B$\flat$–C–D$\flat$–E$\flat$–F–G

D$\flat$ Major: D$\flat$–E$\flat$–F–G$\flat$–A$\flat$–B$\flat$–C

G$\flat$ Major: G$\flat$–A$\flat$–B$\flat$–C$\flat$–D$\flat$–E$\flat$–F

Recommended Listening

Open Chords

"Every Rose Has Its Thorn" – Poison

"Wish You Were Here" – Pink Floyd

"Yesterday" – The Beatles

"More Than Words" – Extreme

Barre Chords

"Space Oddity" – David Bowie

"Long Time" – Boston

"Flake" – Jack Johnson

"I'm Yours" – Jason Mraz

Seventh Chords

"Tears in Heaven" – Eric Clapton

"Mrs. Robinson" – Simon & Garfunkel

"Here Comes the Sun" – The Beatles

"Wonderwall" – Oasis

Other Chord Types

"Free Fallin'" – Tom Petty

"Satellite" – Dave Matthews Band

"3 A.M." – Matchbox Twenty

"Behind Blue Eyes" – The Who

Open-String Drone Chords

"No Excuses" – Alice in Chains

"Closer to Fine" – Indigo Girls

"Hole Hearted" – Extreme

"Breaking the Girl" – Red Hot Chili Peppers